TALE OF A TADPOLE

FIRST EDITION

Series Editor Deborah Lock; **US Senior Editor** Shannon Beatty; **Project Editors** Caroline Bingham, Caryn Jenner, Penny Smith; **Editors** Regina Kahney, Arpita Nath, Anneka Wahlhaus; **Art Editor** Jyotsna Julka, Michelle Baxter; **Senior Art Editor** Ann Cannings; **Producer** Christine Ni; **Senior Producer, Pre-Production** Francesca Wardell; **Picture Researcher** Sakshi Saluja; **Jacket Designer** Hoa Luc; **DTP Designers** Nand Kishor Acharya, Vijay Kandwal, Nityanand Kumar, Anita Yadav; **Managing Editor** Soma B. Chowdhury; **Managing Art Editor** Ahlawat Gunjan; **Art Directors** Rachel Foster, Martin Wilson; **Editorial Consultant** Theresa Greenaway; **Reading Consultant** Linda Gambrell, PhD

THIS EDITION

Editorial Management by Oriel Square
Produced for DK by WonderLab Group LLC
Jennifer Emmett, Erica Green, Kate Hale, *Founders*

Editors Grace Hill Smith, Libby Romero, Michaela Weglinski; **Photography Editors** Kelley Miller, Annette Kiesow, Nicole DiMella; **Managing Editor** Rachel Houghton; **Designers** Project Design Company; **Researcher** Michelle Harris; **Copy Editor** Lori Merritt; **Indexer** Connie Binder; **Proofreader** Larry Shea; **Reading Specialist** Dr. Jennifer Albro; **Curriculum Specialist** Elaine Larson

Published in the United States by DK Publishing
1745 Broadway, 20th Floor, New York, NY 10019

Copyright © 2023 Dorling Kindersley Limited
DK, a Division of Penguin Random House LLC
23 24 25 26 10 9 8 7 6 5 4 3 2 1
001–334010–July/2023

A catalog record for this book
is available from the Library of Congress.
HC ISBN: 978-0-7440-7347-8
PB ISBN: 978-0-7440-7348-5

DK books are available at special discounts when purchased in bulk for sales promotions, premiums, fundraising, or educational use. For details, contact: DK Publishing Special Markets, 1745 Broadway, 20th Floor, New York, NY 10019
SpecialSales@dk.com

Printed and bound in China

The publisher would like to thank the following for their kind permission to reproduce their images:
a=above; c=center; b=below; l=left; r=right; t=top; b/g=background

Dreamstime.com: Manuellacoste 4-5
Cover images: *Front:* **Shutterstock.com:** Kurit afshen br, Claudiu Mihai Badea, Anna Filippenok c, Deborah Lee Rossiter cl

All other images © Dorling Kindersley
For more information see: www.dkimages.com

For the curious
www.dk.com

TALE OF A TADPOLE

Karen Wallace

Contents

The Tadpoles Are Born

The tale of a tadpole begins in a pond. Mother frog lays her eggs next to a lily pad.

Each tiny egg is wrapped
in clear jelly.
A mother frog can lay as many
as 4,000 eggs at once!

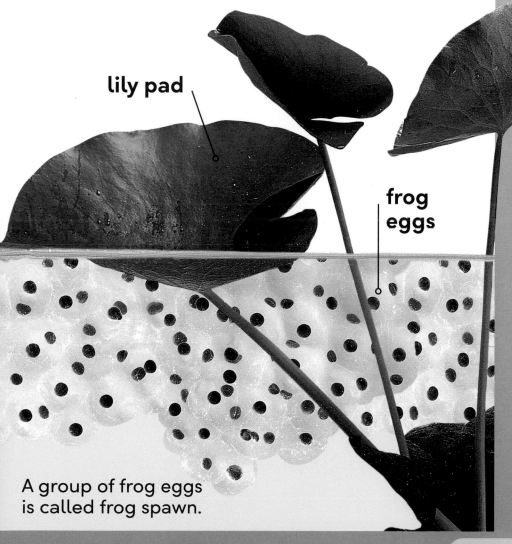

lily pad

frog
eggs

A group of frog eggs
is called frog spawn.

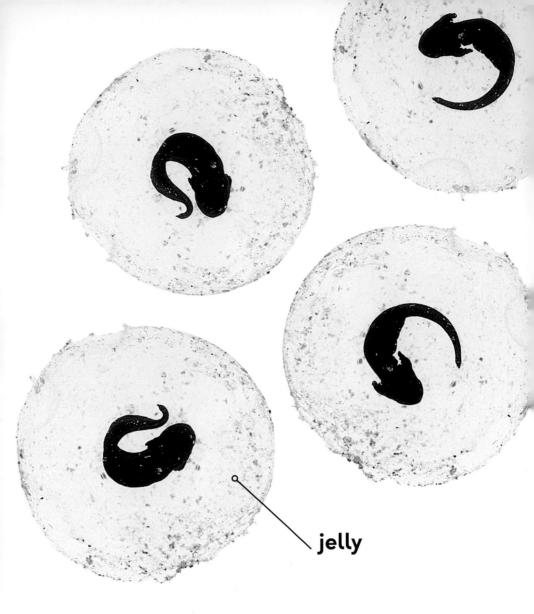

jelly

The egg jelly has food inside
for the growing tadpoles.
The tadpoles wriggle like
worms.

They push through the jelly
and swim in the water.

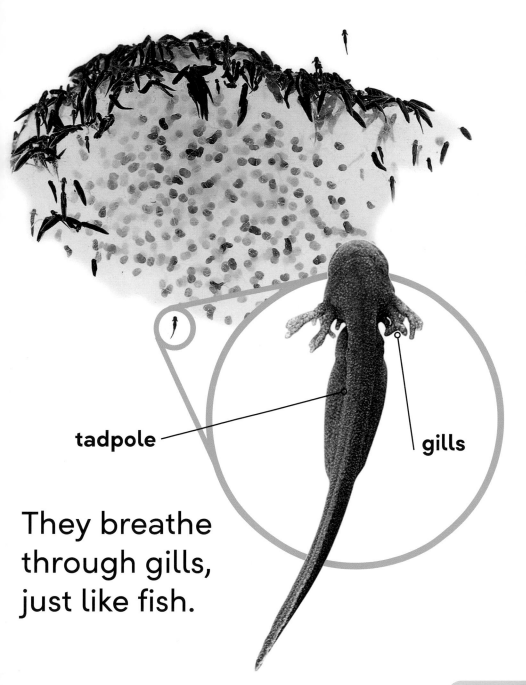

tadpole

gills

They breathe
through gills,
just like fish.

Many other animals
live in the pond.
There are shiny goldfish,
sticklebacks, and great
diving beetles.

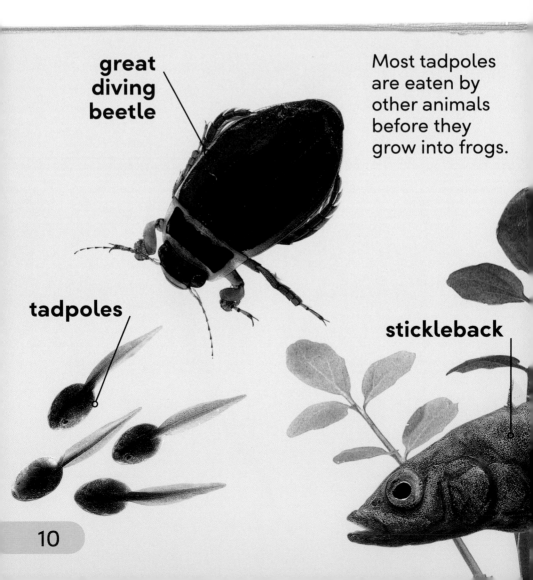

great diving beetle

Most tadpoles
are eaten by
other animals
before they
grow into frogs.

tadpoles

stickleback

They chase the young tadpoles to try to eat them. But the tadpoles wiggle their tails and swim away!

goldfish

Growing Up

Soon a tadpole grows legs with tiny webbed toes.

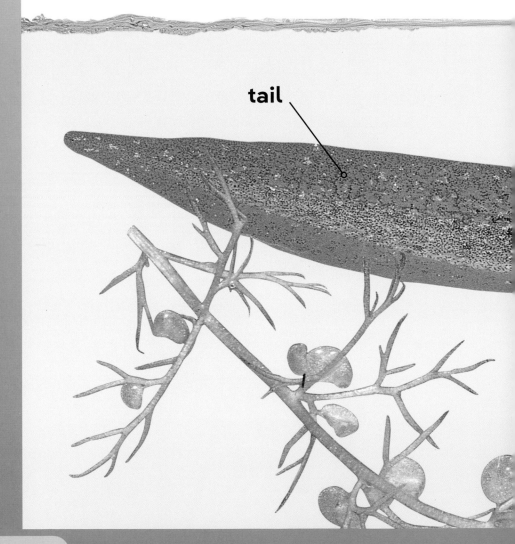

tail

Webbed toes are like flippers.
They help the small tadpole
push through the water.

webbed toes

The tadpole grows front legs
with long, skinny fingers.

It nibbles on plants and gobbles green pondweed.

front
leg

finger

Half tadpole, half frog,
it rests in the sunshine.

Its tail is shrinking.

The tail gets smaller and smaller. Now, the tadpole is nearly a frog.

Life as a Frog

The new little frog
sits on a lily pad.
Its skin is wet and slippery.

nostrils

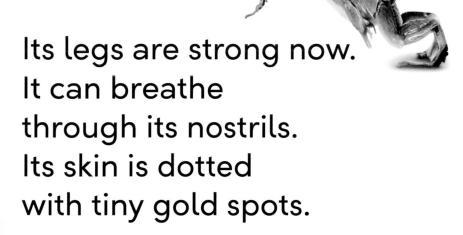

Its legs are strong now.
It can breathe
through its nostrils.
Its skin is dotted
with tiny gold spots.

leg

Frogs must keep their
skin slimy.
This frog hops back in the pond
and swims for a while.
Then it climbs onto a log.

Summer is the best time to spot new adult frogs.

Another frog climbs up
and sits down beside it.
They stay near the water.

Now fully grown, the frog dives through the water.

stickleback

It is not afraid of the stickleback.
It swims past the beetle.

beetle

In the pond, the frog
watches and waits.
What does it see
with its round, beady eyes?

fly

A fly lands
above it.
The frog
creeps closer
and closer.

But another big frog jumps up!
It snatches the fly
with its long, sticky tongue.

The frog
misses its meal.
Next time
it'll be faster!

The golden-skinned frog
chases a dragonfly.
It lands on a lily pad.
Under the lily pad are
hundreds of frogs' eggs.

Inside each egg,
a tadpole is growing.
Each tadpole may grow
into a new frog.

Glossary

Gills
Openings in a tadpole's body that are used to breathe underwater

Jelly
A covering that protects frog eggs

Nostrils
Two openings on a frog's face used to breathe

Tail
The back end of a tadpole's body

Tongue
A long, sticky muscle in a frog's mouth used to catch food

Webbed toe
The skin between toes that helps tadpoles to swim

Index

Quiz

Answer the questions to see what you have learned. Check your answers in the key below.

1. What is wrapped around the tiny frog eggs?

2. What do tadpoles breathe through?

3. Which animals like to eat tadpoles?

4. Which animal has a tail—a tadpole or a frog?

5. What is a group of frog eggs called?

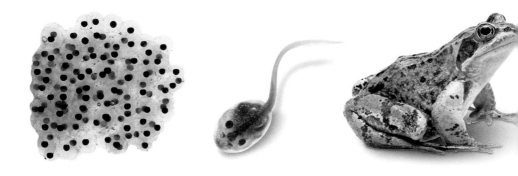

1. Clear jelly 2. Gills 3. Goldfish, sticklebacks, and great diving beetles 4. A tadpole 5. Frog spawn